'Living the Dao'

Louis George Martin.

About this collection

This collection of poems was written in June 2023 during the first Move & Meditate retreat co-hosted by George Thompson and Nathan Gallagher, in which I had the pleasure to serve as a volunteer.

Staying at the 'Crops Not Shops' site in Glastonbury, we lived together as a tribe on the land for 5 days, practicing Tai Qi & Qi Gong every morning and evening, studying the Dao, dancing at sunset, and singing and sharing around the fire late into the night.

This experiential poetry seeks to encapsulate some of the group learning and reflects my own personal and spiritual journey from this magical time.

I hope you find the poems beautiful and inspiring, and that they aid you on your way to the Dao.

A special thank you to all who participated in this retreat and helped to make this such a wonderful and transformational time. Your hearts and words are present here in my words, and will be fondly remembered, always x

The poems herein

1. A friend of the Dao
2. Move and meditate
3. Travelling light
4. A flash of pink
5. A look
6. Those eyes
7. The fire
8. Aurorean
9. A prayer
10. Come together
11. Fire and flow
12. Flies buzzing
13. The perfect eight
14. Morning pages
15. Make hay
16. Not grasping
17. The Dao
18. Tee-hee-hee
19. Mother Earth
20. Lions paw
21. Staring into the flames
22. Haiku

A friend of the Dao

What does it mean to be a friend of the Dao?

What does it mean to be a friend of the now?

Light as a feather floating in the breeze,

I'm here for your joy, to put you at ease,

Surfing the waves on the sea of life,

Wedded to your teacher, the truth, our strife,

Listening to the wind to catch your next move,

As one with the whole you get into the groove,

By the universe hired for the job at hand,

A thousand works of love, the endless demand,

Yet the reward, in truth, is overwhelmingly good,

Eternally blessed, and, at last understood,

The riches that flow from not fighting the show,

But, instead, just abound right here on the ground,

Where you're stood is where you're meant to be,

Just accept it, surrender, you're happy as can be,

Living life in full flow, you're a friend of the Dao,

Eternally present, just living the now.

Move and meditate

'We've just got on the land,'

Arriving here feels like a new beginning,

To answer the call of the Dao,

Is to be of service,

In humility, yet quietly proud, I feel.

People are coming here from all corners of the globe, gathering, to move and meditate, to move and meditate,

It's time to get in the groove, baby,

Living wild on bare feet,

Feeling the scratch of the sun scorched earth,

The grand marquee rippling overhead,

Shading us.

To move is to meditate,

It's a joy to share my practice,

Intuitive chi flow,

Tai Chi,

Qigong,

The dance with life.

Travelling light

Ah, the brevity of being,

That is being unencumbered,

Or lightly so at least,

Setting out to venture with but a simple pack,

Man's feet freed to trek and walk the lonely track,

Best found sure footed in days meant for wandering,

That's why I travel light,

The spirit of an eagle, all dressed up in white.

A flash of pink

A flash of pink curtsies,

Smiling In the high noon sun,

Weathered, old, still young.

'Like the Mona Lisa, but I smile,'

'Mona Lisa, Anna-Lisa,'

She curtsies in her pink floral dress and her weather worn face breaks out into a big grin.

Working the land in her sixties, her hands in the earth, wiry, wearing a bandana.

Such strength and joy –

This is how grandmothers should be.

A look

That look!

A thunderbolt.

They struck at my very soul,

Those grey green eyes and white, white skin,

Pierced me deep, like a dagger plunged into my chest,

They made some kind of incision,

Of that I can be sure,

They've cut a hole in my heart like that,

And now I thirst for more.

Who are they?

This person who happens by,

Dancing on over from across the pond,

And got me all a wondering why,

I always get this way with a pretty face,

These looks…but oh, that look,

The way they looked at me cut me deep,

Like a dagger to the very core,

Now I'm sitting here wondering,

Who are they, who are they, who are they…

Those eyes

To hold your gaze is to hold a waterfall in the palm of my hand,

The eyes they weep, the desire to hold is strong.

How do we accept that which may or may not come to pass?

Aiding those in need,

Sincere in love,

Free of judgement,

Without attachment,

We heed the heart,

Our gifts impart,

In surety of deed,

And when time comes, for you I bleed,

For this true practice –

Art.

The fire

The fire she burns, she burns, she burns, she burns, she burns, she burns,

And everybody learns,

The way as one, forging our truth flames,

Making of selves the hot blade of tempered righteousness,

Welding the terror of the light with the precision of a samurai, the patience of a monk, and the compassion of a priest,

Slash and burn baby, slash and burn...

Left right and centre!

Leave no mortal behind in this immortal race,

Cry forth your voice, pour forth your heart,

The fire of love burning brighter than ever at the centre of your being,

A dazzling star walks the streets,

Writing into the echelons of time the epic nature of your grace,

So let it be told,

So, let us be bold,

Sad, distant, ashamed, locked away –

No more!

The beacon fire has been lit,

The power of now, of belief, of love, held back no more, i beg of thee, I beg of thee,

Let it be so, dear lord,

Upon this mortal crown the weight of the world to bear in your name,

Only walking in your light I can know no burden, only the greatest unparalleled joy,

Do you feel my fire?

Do you feel how I tend to the love in my heart?

Be that gracious keeper of your own fire –

I see a million fires burning brightly on the horizon,

We shall be kept in the dark no more!

The strength of our love is too great!

United as one we live in this blessed age,

The dawning of a new day has come,

Together we live as one, United in this blessed age.

Aurorean

Such is the way of a starry night,

Gathered round in hush and awe,

The voices freed and rising as one great swell,

The beauty of each soul shining as bright as any star,

Spirits lifted towards the heavens,

Hearts melting into harmony,

Come brother, come sister,

Come one, come all, let fly your true beauty,

Take courage, take heart, just begin, it's a start, to learn and grow get going with the flow,

As the night wears on, weary they drift from the fire,

reluctant to surrender the magnificence that has been this day.

But all things come to an end,

Only beginning again,

Always, you are forever, remember,

Singing stars,

The fire kept until dawn,

The lived experience breaking over us, awash with purples, peach and oranges –

Aurorean.

A prayer

The hiss and crackle of a fire burnt down low,

The howling of the dogs,

The ebb and flow of day into night,

As simple as a starry night,

As elegant as a blade of grass,

And as wise as a young boy running naked on the land,

Coming together, I pray, coming together,

May we live and breathe as one,

In eternal harmony, the resplendent truth,

United in our love for God.

Let this be the time,

Let it be now, of all times,

Let it be now.

Let the people come together,

All manmade barriers dissolving into truth,

Living free as it was meant to be,

In truth as I am you,

In joy as you are me.

Come together

I know today with absolute certainty,

That when we all come together as one,

There is not a shred of evil that can stand before us.

You are my greatest strength,

And all the hope I'll ever need,

Come what may, come what may,

When we all come together as one,

There is not a shred of evil that can stand before us.

I feel you all standing here beside me,

Walking hand in hand in paradise,

And in the dawn of this new age,

Finally, finally, all is welcome here on earth,

And there is not a shred of evil that can stand before us.

Fire and flow

The fire has burnt low,

Yet blackened charcoal still remains,

Finely engraved in the earthen pit,

The heavenly dreams and rune forged words,

We seared into the ground and sky above,

Rain clouds breaking with the dawn,

The sun comes again,

And we are ready with our qigong form.

Flies buzzing

Summer solstice approaches,

Flies buzzing round my head,

I don't know what I'm saying,

So, I'll keep silent instead.

The perfect eight

I simply must have my eight,

A perfect whole eight,

When I do, I feel great,

And to date of late I've been having my eight,

Yes, to get in bed, I simply can't wait!

The morning pages

The morning pages are a silly rite,

Oh yes indeed they are,

See how here I waste my time,

When it could be spent in rhyme,

How much better it is,

To spend the day in verse,

In rhythm and flow one should be immersed,

If truly one is to master,

The fine arts of craft and task and thus ever faster,

Do propel towards the end goal though not in sight,

Which is to finally, when all is said and done,

Have alchemised a lump of gold,

From the depths of the iron soul.

Make hay

Make hay while the sun done shine,

Plant crops if ye be a farmer,

Make bread if ye be a baker,

Write words if ye be a poet,

Make hay while sun done shine,

Or lie back, sip the breeze, and make a silly rhyme.

Not grasping

Here comes the moment!

Here it comes!

Wait for it, wait for it,

Now!

It's your turn to speak, go for it!

That thing that's relevant to what's being said, that's burning a hole in your ego to come out,

Say it!

Or,

Just let it go,

Relaxing into silence,

Let the river speak for itself and,

Stop grasping at straws.

The Dao

What to say of the mysterious Dao?

The unknowable thing we call the way,

Of breath and dance and sweet ecstasy,

In he, and pu, and dear Wu Wei,

I'm flattered you even asked me how,

In fact, I've been sitting here all day,

Your happening by, why, pure serendipity,

And this in the asking all's revealed,

Simply sitting, breathing, waiting,

I have found the way!

Tee-hee-hee!

Tee-hee-hee, look at me!

A devilish poet in a yogi's dress,

Take me out on Friday night and out me to the rest,

The dance of life, as always, put here as a test,

You will see with clarity,

I'm as naughty as the rest,

I pray and meditate and do my morning flows,

But I also drink and smoke and trip,

In fact, I am quite free!!!

Mother Earth

Oh, mother earth! Oh, mother earth!

Mother of my children,

We keep asking and you keep giving,

The lessons that we need:

In the bosom of your arm's I am overwhelmed by synchronicity;

A baby by the fireside sung to sleep by the sweet sound of our harmony.

Awaken, oh great dragon!

Awaken, oh great spirit!

Carry me on thy back to the ends of the earth and the ocean,

I will sing of you in the life beyond,

I will forever harken back,

To the blessed days I spent with thee,

Never lonely but United in your company,

This beautiful tribe that sung as one, laughed,

The blessed trees and the numberless children who played, dancing in the sun.

Lion's paw

The beating heart of Zion is the lion's paw,

Hands clasped, Interwoven fingers, a true greeting of the people,

From one generation to the next the torch is passed along the hillside of Methusala,

A shield wall of brothers rooted firm upon the land, calling out our tribal songs against the shadow of the long dark swiftly falling night,

Hearts as wide as the open sky, love pouring forth heavenwards in a Cascading torrent that showers the earth in cinders of fertile joy,

Each tear shed for mankind comes together in a river that blasts away the dams that have held us back for too long!

The beating heart of Zion is the lion's paw,

Tangled dreads sprouting from a rastacap above a finely combed beard, watery corn blue eyes, skin worn and weathered from the sun, and lined with the dirt and sweat of toil.

The lion is fierce, he's got teeth and claws, but the true weapon is courage, a refusal to back down, standing his ground against all comers – pride never to be surrendered.

The enemy comes in suits of war,

Making their case, dressed up in the law,

But whatever they shall bring, we stand ready,

The true strength of Zion,

The beating heart the lion's paw.

Staring into the flames

Ash flecks stir in a spiral – a stray breeze,

These embers that fed on our dreams still warm,

The hour is late my friend, and I feel the silence where you once sat beside me,

Echoing beneath the arches of the bridge between our hearts,

Flying down the viaduct of truth that we built in but a moment,

Sparks of joy kindling this great passion that now stands a bonfire within each heart,

The flames dancing in your eyes,

The fire in each heart for all things lighting the way,

The beacon chain lit across the night sky like a million stars,

The love we've shared a woven constellation, I think I'll name…you,

And I can't help but cry,

Despite the beauty of the here and now,

You took me on a journey through that night sky,

And I find myself waking as if from slumber,

And it seems strange that you are not beside me,

That this bed is cold and empty,

Tells me all I need to know,

The heart sings its own song and I'm listening to the wind,

Straining to catch but a whisper,

The herald of our coming together once more,

Aurorean; roses of all colours catching the sunrise,

This day I can't wait to spend with you,

Shimmers on the horizon, gleaming,

Our friendship a golden treasure,

On a ship that's surely coming into view,

White sails unfurled, and flying in the wind, homeward bound with tales of the beyond,

I sit here on the sandy shore, and I wait, I wait, for you, I wait.

Haiku

Movement snack – jump up!

Relentless – the whip of self,

Onwards dogs, we cry!

Love beyond the shell,

Truly seeing who you are,

Lights me up inside.

Sweet effortless being,

Bow to the divine within,

Breathe in harmony.

Softness equals strength,

The river roars like thunder,

And slips slowly by.

Flow is the key word,

We are truly all we need,

In the Dao we trust.

To act as the leaf,

You must turn towards the sun,

Dancing in the wind,

Be at one with thunder,

the ripples come from a drop,

True peace is within,

Weary pilgrims seek,

Healing, shelter, peace and love,

The tree stands alone.

There is no perfection,

There is no escape,

There is only the eternal storm,

Narrative rains,

To burn yourself with cruel words

Or will you show mercy?

Water gods garden,

Eat, drink, pray, and be merry,

Life shall nurture life,

The double-edged sword

Hurting or defending right

Taking care with words,

To learn of dear Wu Wei,

Ah, the inner mountain view,

Responsibility.

Ah, enlightenment,

Not freedom from, freedom to,

Nourished by silence.

If you're feeling low,

Only take one step outside,

So, are you ready?

God, I ask of you,

Nothing, but let me love you,

And all the good things.

Letter of thanks

A deep gratitude to my friend George who invited me to come on this retreat and allowed me to help out as a volunteer. Your personal ethos, creative playful energy, powerful drive, unreal talent, generosity of heart and soul, and dedication to your cause, is a constant source of inspiration. To my new friend Nathan, I adore the Lovejam conscious community that you've built. It's changed my life in so many ways for the better, and it was wonderful for me to be a part of one of your events. The spirit, the love, the effort that was put into this retreat was an inspiration, and being a part of the incredible team of radiant humans that you brought together humbled me.

For the land in Glastonbury at *'Crops Not Shops'* which continues to welcome me. Every time I'm there I want to accept your open-hearted invitation to come and live on the land in tribe with your beautiful souls. Your work is amazing, Chay and Co. Picking food straight from the land to go in our salads could not have been more wholesome. You are a shining example to us all, leading the way forward in these difficult times and showing that it can be done. There is another way that does not involve the death of the planet: permaculture, regenerative farming, and escaping consumerism.

To all those who came to the retreat and shared from a place of vulnerability and open heartedness, thank you. The transformation here was very real, profound, and I feel the ripples still reaching out effecting change in all who feel their touch. There is always so much to say, but I want to keep it simple: you help me be the best version of myself. The light of my heart burns brighter, and I hope you will look for me in the night sky.

Finally, a special thanks to the other volunteers Jen, Moana, Nina Backhouse, and Benedick –

Singing naked with you in the white spring was a deep spiritual moment I will treasure forever and drumming all night at Stonehenge on the solstice a few days later, unforgettable. What. A. Team.

There were so many special moments during this time, you all know who you are, and you know I love you all.

Yours faithfully,

Louis George Martin.

Printed in Great Britain
by Amazon